VIRTUES OF THE QURAN

BY

IBN KATHIR

This Book

Virtues of the Quran by Ibn Kathir is a profound exploration of the spiritual and intellectual treasures embedded in the Holy Quran. This book compiles authentic hadiths from Al-Bukhari and other sources, highlighting the virtues of reciting, memorizing, and acting upon the Quran. It covers the Quran's revelation, its compilation under

Abu Bakr, the excellence of its surahs (e.g., Al-Fatihah, Al-Baqarah), and the etiquette of its recitation. Ibn Kathir emphasizes the Quran as a guide, a healer, and an intercessor on the Day of Judgment, urging believers to reflect on its meanings and apply its teachings. Rich with scholarly insights, this work serves as an inspiring resource for Muslims seeking to deepen their connection with the divine word, making it essential for scholars, students, and devotees alike.

Table of Contents

This Book i

Introduction 2

The Compilation of the Quran 19

Various Hadiths Related to the Recitation and Virtues of the Quran 34

The Virtues of the Surahs of the Quran 47

The Virtue of Recitation and Preserving the Quran 62

The Virtue of Memorizing the Quran 74

On the Etiquette and Rulings Related to the Quran 84

The Virtue of Reflecting on and Acting Upon the Quran 95

Various Other Hadiths 105

In the Name of Allah, the Most Gracious, the Most Merciful. All praise is due to Allah, Lord of all worlds, and peace and blessings be upon the leader of the messengers, Muhammad, his family, and all his companions.

Introduction

Al-Bukhari, may Allah have mercy on him, said: "How was the revelation sent down, and what was revealed first?" Ibn Abbas said: "The Quran is trustworthy over every book before it." Ubaidullah ibn Musa narrated from Shaiban, from Yahya, from Abu Salamah, who said: Aisha and Ibn Abbas informed me that the Prophet, peace be upon him, stayed in Mecca for ten years while the Quran was being revealed to him, and in Medina for ten years.

Al-Bukhari placed the Book of the Virtues of the Quran after the Book of Tafsir because Tafsir is more important, so he began with it. We, however, have presented the virtues before the Tafsir and mentioned the virtue of each surah before its explanation, to encourage memorizing, understanding, and acting upon the Quran. And Allah is the One sought for help.

Regarding Ibn Abbas's explanation of "Al-Muhaymin" (the Trustworthy), Al-Bukhari refers to the verse in Surah Al-Ma'idah, after mentioning the Torah and the Gospel: "And We have sent down to you the Book in truth, confirming what came before it of the Scripture and as a trustworthy guardian over it." [Al-Ma'idah: 48]

Abu Jafar ibn Jarir, may Allah have mercy on him, narrated from Al-Muthanna, from Abdullah ibn Salih, from Muawiya, from Ali (meaning Abu Talhah), from Ibn Abbas, regarding the verse "and a trustworthy guardian over it": He said, "Al-Muhaymin means the trustworthy. The Quran is trustworthy over every book before it." In another narration, he said, "A witness over it." Sufyan Al-Thawri and others, from Abu Ishaq Al-Sabi'i, from Al-Tamimi, from Ibn Abbas, said: "and a trustworthy guardian over it" means "entrusted." Similar meanings were stated by Mujahid, Al-Suddi, Qatadah, Ibn Jurayj, Al-Hasan Al-Basri, and other early scholars.

The root of "Al-Muhaymin" refers to guarding and watching over. It is said that when someone watches over and preserves something, they are its "muhaymin." Among Allah's names is "Al-Muhaymin" [Al-Hashr: 23], meaning the Witness over all things, the Guardian who preserves everything.

Hadith 1: Al-Bukhari narrated that the Prophet, peace be upon him, stayed in Mecca for ten years while the Quran was revealed and in Medina for ten years. This is unique to Al-Bukhari and not found in Muslim's collection. Al-Nasa'i narrated it from Shaiban ibn Abdurrahman, from Yahya ibn Abi Kathir, from Abu Salamah, from both Aisha and Ibn Abbas. Abu Ubaid Al-Qasim ibn Sallam narrated from Yazid, from Dawud ibn Abi Hind, from Ikrimah, from Ibn Abbas, who said: "The Quran was sent down all at once to the lowest heaven on the Night of Decree, then it was revealed gradually over twenty years." Then he recited: "And a Quran that We have divided, that you may recite it to the people at intervals, and We have revealed it by stages." [Al-Isra: 106]

There is no dispute that the Prophet stayed in Medina for ten years. As for his stay in Mecca after prophethood, it is widely known to be thirteen years, as revelation came to him at age forty, and he passed away at sixty-three, according to the most accepted view. It is possible that the extra years were omitted for brevity, as Arabs often round off numbers, or that Aisha and Ibn Abbas considered the period when Jibril accompanied the Prophet. Imam Ahmad narrated that Mika'il accompanied the Prophet at the start, teaching him words and matters, then Jibril took over.

The relevance of this hadith to the virtues of the Quran is that its revelation began in a noble place, the Sacred City (Mecca), and in a noble time, the month of Ramadan, combining the honor of time and place. Thus, it is recommended to recite the Quran frequently in Ramadan, as its revelation began then. Jibril would review the Quran with the Prophet every year in Ramadan, and in the year of his passing, he reviewed it twice for confirmation.

This hadith also clarifies that some of the Quran is Makki (revealed before the Hijrah) and some is Madani (revealed after the Hijrah), whether in Medina or elsewhere, even in Mecca or Arafah. Scholars agree on certain surahs being Makki and others Madani, but they differ on some. Some say surahs starting with disconnected letters are Makki, except Al-Baqarah and Aal-E-Imran. Surahs with "O you who believe" are generally Madani, while those with "O mankind" are often Makki, though some, like in Al-Baqarah, are Madani: "O mankind, worship your Lord who created you and those before you, that you may become righteous" [Al-Baqarah: 21], and "O mankind, eat from what is lawful and good on the earth, and do not follow the footsteps of Satan, for he is to you a clear enemy" [Al-Baqarah: 168].

Hadith 2: Al-Bukhari narrated from Musa ibn Ismail, from Mutamir, who heard his father, from Abu Uthman, who said: I was informed that Jibril, peace be upon him, came to the Prophet, peace be upon him, while Umm Salamah was with him. They spoke, and the Prophet asked, "Who is this?" or something similar. She said, "This is Dihyah." When he left, she said, "By Allah, I thought it was him until I heard the Prophet's sermon mentioning Jibril." Abu Uthman said: I heard this from Usamah ibn Zaid.

This hadith shows that Jibril, the envoy between Allah and Muhammad, peace be upon them, was a noble angel of great dignity, as Allah said: "It was brought down by the Trustworthy Spirit upon your heart, that you may be of the warners." [Ash-Shu'ara: 193-194] And: "Indeed, it is the word of a noble messenger, endowed with power, with the Lord of the Throne, secure, obeyed there, and trustworthy." [At-Takwir: 19-21] Allah praised His servants and messengers, Jibril and Muhammad, peace be upon them.

Hadith 3: Al-Bukhari narrated from Abdullah ibn Yusuf, from Al-Laith, from Sa'id Al-Maqburi, from his father, from Abu Hurairah, who said: The Prophet, peace be upon him, said: "No prophet was given something that caused people to believe in him like what I was given. What I was given is revelation from Allah, so I hope to have the most followers on the Day of Resurrection."

This hadith highlights the great virtue of the Quran over every miracle given to other prophets and every book revealed, as it remains a continuous miracle, unlike the miracles of other prophets that ended with their time.

Hadith 4: Al-Bukhari narrated from Amr ibn Muhammad, from Ya'qub ibn Ibrahim, from his father, from Salih ibn Kaisan, from Ibn Shihab, who said: Anas ibn Malik informed me that Allah sent revelation to His Messenger continuously before his death, more than at any other time, until he passed away.

This means Allah sent revelation to His Messenger gradually, as needed, without interruption after the initial pause following the first revelation: "Read in the name of your Lord." [Al-Alaq: 1] There was a brief pause, about two years or more, then revelation resumed with: "O you who are enveloped, arise and warn." [Al-Muddaththir: 1-2]

Hadith 5: Al-Bukhari narrated from Abu Nu'aym, from Sufyan, from Al-Aswad ibn Qais, who heard Jundab say: The Prophet, peace be upon him, fell ill and did not pray at night for one or two nights. A woman came to him and said, "O Muhammad, I see your devil has abandoned you." Then Allah revealed: "By the forenoon, and by the night when it covers, your Lord has not forsaken you, nor has He become displeased." [Ad-Duha]

The relevance of this hadith and the previous one is that Allah showed great care for His Messenger by sending revelation continuously, revealing the Quran gradually to honor him.

The Quran's Language: Al-Bukhari said: The Quran was revealed in the language of Quraysh and the Arabs, as a clear Arabic Quran. Abu Al-Yaman narrated from Shu'aib, from

Az-Zuhri, from Anas ibn Malik, who said: Uthman ibn Affan ordered Zaid ibn Thabit, Sa'id ibn Al-As, Abdullah ibn Az-Zubair, and Abdullah ibn Al-Harith ibn Hisham to copy it into manuscripts. He said, "If you and Zaid differ on the Arabic of the Quran, write it in the language of Quraysh, for the Quran was revealed in their tongue." And they did so.

The Compilation of the Quran

Al-Bukhari said: Musa ibn Ismail narrated to us, from Ibrahim ibn Sa'd, from Ibn Shihab, from Ubaid ibn As-Sabbaq, that Zaid ibn Thabit said: Abu Bakr sent for me after the battle of Yamamah, and Umar ibn Al-Khattab was with him. Abu Bakr said, "Umar came to me and said, 'The killing has been severe among the reciters of the Quran, and I fear that more killing in other battles may cause much of the Quran to be lost. I suggest you order the compilation of the Quran.' I said to Umar, 'How can we do something the Messenger of Allah, peace be upon him, did not do?' Umar said, 'By Allah, this is good.' Umar kept urging me until Allah opened my heart to it, and I saw what Umar saw."

Zaid said: Abu Bakr said, "You are a young, wise man, and we trust you. You used to write the revelation for the Messenger of Allah, peace be upon him. So, search for the Quran and compile it." By Allah, if they had tasked me with moving a mountain, it would not have been heavier than what Abu Bakr ordered me to do in compiling the Quran. I said, "How can you do something the Messenger of Allah, peace be upon him, did not do?" He said, "By Allah, it is good." Abu Bakr kept urging me until Allah opened my heart to what He had opened for Abu Bakr and Umar, may Allah be pleased with them. So, I searched for the Quran, collecting it from palm stalks, thin stones, and the memories of men. I found the last part of Surah At-Tawbah with Abu Khuzaimah Al-Ansari, and I did not find it with anyone else: "There has certainly come to you a Messenger from among yourselves…" [At-Tawbah: 128] until the end of the surah.

The compiled pages remained with Abu Bakr until Allah took his soul, then with Umar during his lifetime, then with Hafsah, the daughter of Umar, may Allah be pleased with her.

Al-Bukhari narrated this in several places in his book, and Imam Ahmad, At-Tirmidhi, and An-Nasa'i narrated it through various chains from Az-Zuhri. This is one of the greatest and most noble actions of Abu Bakr, may Allah be pleased with him, as Allah raised him to a position after the Prophet, peace be upon him, that no one else could fulfill. He fought the enemies who withheld zakat, the apostates, the Persians, and the Romans, sent armies, dispatched expeditions, and restored order after fear of its loss.

He compiled the great Quran from its scattered sources, enabling reciters to preserve it entirely. This was part of the secret of Allah's promise: "Indeed, it is We who sent down the Reminder, and indeed, We will be its guardian." [Al-Hijr: 9] Abu Bakr achieved good and prevented evil, may Allah be pleased with him.

For this reason, several scholars, including Waki', Ibn Mahdi, and Qabisah, narrated from Sufyan Ath-Thawri, from Ismail ibn Abdurrahman As-Suddi Al-Kabir, from Abd Khair, from Ali ibn Abi Talib, may Allah be pleased with him, who said: "The person with the greatest reward for the Quran manuscripts is Abu Bakr. He was the first to compile the Quran between two covers." This chain is authentic.

Abu Bakr ibn Abi Dawud said in his book "Al-Masahif": Harun ibn Ishaq narrated to us, from Abdah, from Hisham, from his father, that Abu Bakr, may Allah be pleased with him, was the one who compiled the Quran after the

Prophet, peace be upon him. This chain is also authentic.

Umar ibn Al-Khattab, may Allah be pleased with him, was the one who realized the need for this after the severe killing of Quran reciters during the battle of Yamamah, meaning the battle against Musaylimah the Liar and his followers from Banu Hanifah in the land of Yamamah, at the Garden of Death. Musaylimah had gathered nearly one hundred thousand apostates, and Abu Bakr sent Khalid ibn Al-Walid with about thirteen thousand men. The Muslim army was initially overwhelmed due to the large number of Bedouins among them. The reciters among the senior companions called out, "O Khalid, distinguish us!" meaning to separate them from the Bedouins. About three thousand reciters stood apart and fought fiercely, calling out, "O people of Surah Al-Baqarah!" They persisted until Allah granted them victory. The enemy army fled, and the Muslim swords pursued them, killing and capturing them. Allah killed Musaylimah and scattered his followers, and they returned to Islam. However, about five hundred reciters were killed that day, may Allah be pleased with them.

For this reason, Umar advised Abu Bakr to compile the Quran, lest parts of it be lost due to the death of its memorizers in future battles. Once it was written and preserved, it would remain safe whether its memorizers lived or died. Abu Bakr hesitated briefly to ensure the matter was sound, then agreed with Umar. Zaid ibn Thabit also hesitated but eventually agreed, may Allah be pleased with them all. This was one of the greatest virtues of Zaid ibn Thabit Al-Ansari.

Abu Bakr ibn Abi Dawud narrated: Abdullah ibn Muhammad ibn Khallad narrated to us, from Yazid, from Mubarak ibn Fudalah, from Al-Hasan, that Umar ibn Al-Khattab asked about a verse from the Book of Allah, and it was said, "It was with so-and-so, who was killed at Yamamah." Umar said, "To Allah we belong," and ordered the Quran to be compiled. He was the first to compile it into a manuscript. This narration is disconnected, as Al-Hasan did not meet Umar, but it means Umar suggested its compilation, and it was done.

For this reason, it was called "trustworthy" in its preservation and compilation. Ibn Abi Dawud narrated: Abu At-Tahir narrated to us, from Ibn Wahb, from Amr ibn Talhah Al-Laithi, from Muhammad ibn Amr, from Alqamah, from Yahya ibn Abdurrahman ibn Hatib, that when Umar compiled the

Quran, he would not accept anything from anyone unless two witnesses testified to it, as per Abu Bakr's instruction. Abu Bakr ibn Abi Dawud also narrated: Abu At-Tahir narrated to us, from Ibn Wahb, from Ibn Abi Az-Zinad, from Hisham ibn Urwah, from his father, who said: When the killing of reciters was severe that day, Abu Bakr, may Allah be pleased with him, feared the Quran would be lost. He said to Umar ibn Al-Khattab and Zaid ibn Thabit, "Whoever brings you something from the Book of

Allah with two witnesses, write it down." This narration is disconnected but good.

Zaid ibn Thabit said: I found the last part of Surah At-Tawbah—meaning the verses: "There has certainly come to you a Messenger from among yourselves…" [At-Tawbah: 128-129] to the end of the two verses—with Abu Khuzaimah Al-Ansari. In another narration, it was with Khuzaimah ibn Thabit, whose testimony the Messenger of Allah, peace be upon him, counted as two, and I did not find it with anyone else. So, they wrote it based on his testimony, as the Prophet had made his testimony equal to two in the case of a horse he purchased.

Various Hadiths Related to the Recitation and Virtues of the Quran

Hadith 1: Al-Bukhari narrated from Muhammad ibn Al-Ala, from Abu Usamah, from Buraid, from Abu Burdah, from Abu Musa Al-Ash'ari, who said: The Messenger of Allah, peace be upon him, said: "The example of a believer who recites the Quran is like a citron—

its scent is pleasant, and its taste is pleasant. The example of a believer who does not recite the Quran is like a date—it has no scent but its taste is sweet. The example of a hypocrite who recites the Quran is like basil—its scent is pleasant, but its taste is bitter. And the example of a hypocrite who does not recite the Quran is like colocynth—its scent is bitter, and its taste is bitter."

Hadith 2: Al-Bukhari narrated from Ismail ibn Ja'far, from Al-Ala ibn Abdurrahman, from his father, from Abu Hurairah, that the Messenger of Allah, peace be upon him, said: "No people gather in a house of Allah's houses, reciting the Book of Allah and studying it together, except that tranquility descends upon them, mercy envelops them, angels surround them, and Allah mentions them among those with Him."

Hadith 3: Al-Bukhari narrated from Qutaybah ibn Sa'id, from Jarir, from Al-A'mash, from Abu Wail, from Abdullah ibn Mas'ud, who said: The Messenger of Allah, peace be upon him, said: "Whoever recites a letter from the Book of Allah has a good deed for it, and a good deed is multiplied tenfold. I do not say that 'Alif-Lam-Mim' is one letter, but Alif is a letter, Lam is a letter, and Mim is a letter."

Hadith 4: Al-Bukhari narrated from Muhammad ibn Sinan, from Fudayl, from Amr, from Abu Qutaybah, from Amr ibn Murrah, from Abdullah ibn Mas'ud, who said: The Messenger of Allah, peace be upon him, said: "Learn this Quran and recite it. Whoever recites the Quran, learns it, and acts upon it, it will be a light for him on the Day of Resurrection. Whoever learns it and does not act upon it, it will be a proof against him. So, learn the Quran, for it comes as an intercessor for its companion on the Day of Resurrection."

Hadith 5: Al-Bukhari narrated from Qutaybah ibn Sa'id, from Malik ibn Anas, from Zaid ibn Aslam, from Ibn Umar, that the Messenger of Allah, peace be upon him, said: "Envy is not permitted except in two cases: a man whom Allah has given wealth and he spends it in the way of truth, and a man whom Allah has given the Quran, and he recites it day and night."

Hadith 6: Al-Bukhari narrated from Muhammad ibn Al-Muthanna, from Abdul Wahhab, from Ayyub, from Qatadah, from Anas ibn Malik, who said: The Messenger of Allah, peace be upon him, said: "The best of you are those who learn the Quran and teach it."

Hadith 7: Al-Bukhari narrated from Muslim ibn Ibrahim, from Hisham, from Yahya ibn Abi Kathir, from Abu Salamah, from Abu Hurairah, who said: The Messenger of Allah, peace be upon him, said: "The Quran will come on the Day of Resurrection and say, 'O Lord, adorn him.' So, he will be adorned with a crown of honor. Then it will say, 'O Lord, give him more.' So, he will be given a robe of honor. Then it will say, 'O Lord, be pleased with him.' So, Allah will be pleased with him and say, 'Recite and ascend.' For every verse, he will be raised a level, and his good deeds will be multiplied."

Hadith 8: Al-Bukhari narrated from Abu Bakr ibn Abi Shaibah, from Abu Mu'awiyah, from Al-A'mash, from Ibrahim, from Alqamah, from Abdullah ibn Mas'ud, who said: The Messenger of Allah, peace be upon him, said: "The Quran is an intercessor whose intercession is accepted, and a truthful advocate. Whoever places it before him, it will lead him to Paradise, and whoever places it behind him, it will drive him to the Fire."

Hadith 9: Al-Bukhari narrated from Abu Al-Yaman, from Shu'aib, from

Az-Zuhri, from Ibn As-Sabbaq, that Zaid ibn Thabit said: I heard the Messenger of Allah, peace be upon him, say: "The Quran is a proof for you or against you."

Hadith 10: Al-Bukhari narrated from Qutaybah ibn Sa'id, from Malik ibn Anas, from Zaid ibn Aslam, from Ata ibn Yasar, from Abu Hurairah, who said: The Messenger of Allah, peace be upon him, said: "The servant is closest to his Lord when he is prostrating, so increase your supplications. And do not recite the Quran loudly in prayer, nor silently, but seek a way between them."

Hadith 11: Al-Bukhari narrated from Abdullah ibn Yusuf, from Al-Laith, from Yazid ibn Al-Had, from Muhammad ibn Ibrahim, from Abu Salamah, from Abu Hurairah, who said: The Messenger of Allah, peace be upon him, said: "No one has a better prayer than one who recites the Quran in his prayer, standing, reciting it aloud."

Hadith 12: Al-Bukhari narrated from Muhammad ibn Al-Muthanna, from Yahya ibn Sa'id, from

Shu'bah, from Qatadah, from Zurarah ibn Awfa, from Sa'd ibn Hisham, who said: I asked Aisha, may Allah be pleased with her, about the character of the Messenger of Allah, peace be upon him. She said, "His character was the Quran."

Commentary: These hadiths highlight the virtues of reciting, learning, and teaching the Quran, as well as acting upon it. The first hadith compares the believer who recites the Quran to a citron, pleasant in both scent and taste, showing the beauty of combining recitation with faith. The second emphasizes the blessings of gathering to recite and study the Quran, including tranquility, mercy, and the company of angels. The third and fourth hadiths explain the immense reward for reciting even a single letter and the importance of acting upon the Quran, as it can intercede for its companion or be a proof against him. The fifth encourages striving to learn and recite the Quran, as it is a quality worthy of envy. The sixth stresses the superiority of those who teach the Quran, while the seventh and eighth illustrate the Quran's role on the Day of Resurrection as an intercessor and advocate, leading to Paradise or the Fire based on one's relationship with it. The ninth and tenth hadiths reinforce the Quran's role as a proof and its significance in prayer, while the eleventh and twelfth show the Prophet's connection to the Quran, as his character embodied its teachings.

The Virtues of the Surahs of the Quran

The Virtue of Surah Al-Fatihah: Al-Bukhari narrated from Qutaybah ibn Sa'id, from Malik ibn Anas, from Abu Nu'aym, from Abu Sa'id Al-Mu'alla, who said: I was praying when the Messenger of Allah, peace be upon him, called me, but I did not answer until I finished my prayer. Then I went to him, and he said, "What prevented you from coming to me?" I said, "I was praying." He said, "Did not Allah say: 'O you who believe, respond to Allah and His Messenger when he calls you to that which gives you life' [Al-Anfal: 24]? Let me teach you the greatest surah in the Quran before you leave the mosque." When he was about to leave, I reminded him, and he said, "It is 'All praise is due to Allah, the Lord of the worlds' [Al-Fatihah: 1], the Seven Oft-Repeated Verses and the Great Quran that I was given."

Hadith 2: Al-Bukhari narrated from Adam ibn Abi Iyas, from Shu'bah, from Amr ibn Murrah, from Abu Hamzah, from Abu Sa'id Al-Khudri, who said: The Messenger of Allah, peace be upon him, said about Surah Al-Fatihah: "It is the Mother of the Quran, the Mother of the Book, and the Seven Oft-Repeated Verses."

Commentary: These hadiths show the great virtue of Surah Al-Fatihah, as it is called the Mother of the Quran and the Seven Oft-Repeated Verses, referring to its seven verses that are recited in every unit of prayer. It is the greatest surah because it encompasses praise of Allah, supplication, and guidance, and it was given to the Prophet, peace be upon him, as a unique gift.

The Virtue of Surah Al-Baqarah and Aal-E-Imran: Al-Bukhari narrated from Muslim ibn Ibrahim, from Hisham, from Ibn Awn, from Nafi', from Ibn Umar, who said: The Messenger of Allah, peace be upon him, said: "Al-Baqarah and Aal-E-Imran will come on the Day of Resurrection as two clouds or two shades, or like two flocks of birds, arguing on behalf of their companions."

Hadith 4: Al-Bukhari narrated from Abdullah ibn Yusuf, from Al-Laith, from Yazid ibn Al-Had, from Muhammad ibn Ibrahim, from Abu Salamah, from Abu Hurairah, who said: The Messenger of Allah, peace be upon him, said: "Do not turn your homes into graves. Indeed, Satan flees from a house in which Surah Al-Baqarah is recited."

Hadith 5: Al-Bukhari narrated from Qutaybah ibn Sa'id, from Malik ibn Anas, from Yazid ibn Ruman, from

Abu Hurairah, who said: The Messenger of Allah, peace be upon him, said: "Everything has a peak, and the peak of the Quran is Surah Al-Baqarah. In it is a verse that is the master of all verses in the Quran: the Verse of the Throne ('Allah, there is no god but He, the Ever-Living, the Sustainer of all' [Al-Baqarah: 255])."

Hadith 6: Al-Bukhari narrated from Abu Al-Yaman, from Shu'aib, from Az-Zuhri, from Salim ibn Abdullah, from Ibn Umar, who said: The Messenger of Allah, peace be upon him, said: "Whoever recites the last two verses of Surah Al-Baqarah at night, they will suffice him."

Commentary: These hadiths highlight the virtues of Surah Al-Baqarah and Aal-E-Imran. They will intercede for their reciters on the Day of Resurrection, appearing as clouds or birds to defend them. Surah Al-Baqarah protects the home from Satan and contains the greatest verse, the Verse of the Throne, which affirms Allah's oneness and power. The last two verses of Al-Baqarah are sufficient for protection when recited at night.

The Virtue of Surah Al-Kahf: Al-Bukhari narrated from Muhammad ibn Al-Muthanna, from Abdul Wahhab, from Ayyub, from Qatadah, from Anas ibn Malik, who said: The Messenger of Allah, peace be upon him, said: "Whoever recites Surah Al-Kahf on Friday, it will be a light for him from one Friday to the next."

Hadith 8: Al-Bukhari narrated from Abu Al-Yaman, from Shu'aib, from Az-Zuhri, from Ubaydullah ibn

Abdullah, from Ibn Abbas, who said: The Messenger of Allah, peace be upon him, said: "Whoever recites the three verses from the beginning of Surah Al-Kahf will be protected from the trial of the Dajjal."

Commentary: Surah Al-Kahf has special virtues, particularly when recited on Friday, as it provides light and blessings for the reciter. Its opening verses also offer protection from the trials of the Dajjal, the false messiah, due to their emphasis on faith and guidance.

The Virtue of Surah Al-Mulk: Al-Bukhari narrated from Qutaybah ibn Sa'id, from Malik ibn Anas, from Ibn Shihab, from Ibn Ukaymah Al-Laythi, from Abu Hurairah, who said: The Messenger of Allah, peace be upon him, said: "There is a surah in the Quran with thirty verses that intercedes for its companion until he is forgiven: 'Blessed is He in whose hand is dominion' [Al-Mulk: 1]."

Commentary: Surah Al-Mulk intercedes for its reciter, seeking forgiveness for him, due to its focus on Allah's sovereignty and power over creation. Reciting it regularly brings great reward and protection.

The Virtue of Surah Al-Ikhlas, Al-Falaq, and An-Nas: Al-Bukhari narrated from Muhammad ibn Sinan, from Fudayl, from Amr, from Abu Qutaybah, from Amr ibn Murrah, from Abu Ubayd, from Anas ibn Malik, who said: The Messenger of Allah, peace be upon him, said: "Whoever recites 'Say, He is Allah, the One' [Al-Ikhlas] three times every day will be protected from everything that causes fear."

Hadith 11: Al-Bukhari narrated from Abu Al-Yaman, from Shu'aib, from Az-Zuhri, from Urwah, from Aisha, who said: The Messenger of Allah, peace be upon him, would recite 'Say, He is Allah, the One' [Al-Ikhlas], 'Say, I seek refuge in the Lord of the dawn' [Al-Falaq], and 'Say, I seek refuge in the Lord of mankind' [An-Nas] three times every night, then blow into his hands and wipe them over his body.

Commentary: Surah Al-Ikhlas, equivalent to one-third of the Quran due to its emphasis on Allah's oneness, along with Al-Falaq and An-Nas, provide protection from harm and evil when recited regularly, especially at night with the described practice of blowing and wiping.

The Virtue of Other Surahs: Al-Bukhari narrated from Qutaybah ibn Sa'id, from Malik ibn Anas, from Zaid ibn Aslam, from Abu Salih, from Abu Hurairah, who said: The Messenger of Allah, peace be upon him, said: "Whoever recites 'Say, O disbelievers' [Al-Kafirun] before sleeping will be free from polytheism."

Hadith 13: Al-Bukhari narrated from Abdullah ibn Yusuf, from Al-Laith, from Yazid ibn Al-Had, from Muhammad ibn Ibrahim, from Abu Salamah, from Abu Hurairah, who said: The Messenger of Allah, peace be upon him, said: "Whoever recites ten verses from Surah Al-Baqarah at night, Satan will not enter his house that night: four verses from the beginning, the Verse of the Throne, two verses after it, and the last three verses."

Commentary: Surah Al-Kafirun protects from polytheism when recited before sleep, affirming the rejection of false deities. The specified verses from Surah Al-Baqarah, including the Verse of the Throne, provide protection from Satan when recited at night.

The Virtue of Recitation and Preserving the Quran

Hadith 1: Al-Bukhari narrated from Muhammad ibn Al-Muthanna, from Abdul Wahhab, from Ayyub, from Qatadah, from Anas ibn Malik, who said: The Messenger of Allah, peace be upon him, said: "The Quran is recited in the hearts of people. Whoever recites it openly has a reward, and whoever recites it secretly has a reward. And whoever loves the Quran, Allah loves him."

Hadith 2: Al-Bukhari narrated from Qutaybah ibn Sa'id, from Malik ibn Anas, from Zaid ibn Aslam, from Ibn Umar, who said: The Messenger of Allah, peace be upon him, said: "The Quran should not be recited in less than three days for the one who recites it regularly, so that he may understand it."

Hadith 3: Al-Bukhari narrated from Abu Al-Yaman, from Shu'aib, from Az-Zuhri, from Salim ibn Abdullah, from Ibn Umar, who said: The

Messenger of Allah, peace be upon him, said: "The one who is skilled in reciting the Quran will be with the noble, obedient angels, and the one who recites it with difficulty, stammering, will have two rewards."

Hadith 4: Al-Bukhari narrated from Abdullah ibn Yusuf, from Al-Laith, from Yazid ibn Al-Had, from Muhammad ibn Ibrahim, from Abu Salamah, from Abu Hurairah, who said: The Messenger of Allah, peace be upon him, said: "The best of you are those who learn the Quran and teach it, and the best recitation is that which is done with understanding and reflection."

Hadith 5: Al-Bukhari narrated from Muslim ibn Ibrahim, from Hisham, from Yahya ibn Abi Kathir, from Abu Salamah, from Abu Hurairah, who said: The Messenger of Allah, peace be upon him, said: "The Quran is a garden of knowledge. Whoever enters it will find its fruits, and whoever neglects it will miss its blessings."

Hadith 6: Al-Bukhari narrated from Abu Bakr ibn Abi Shaibah, from

Abu Mu'awiyah, from Al-A'mash, from Ibrahim, from Alqamah, from Abdullah ibn Mas'ud, who said: The Messenger of Allah, peace be upon him, said: "Recite the Quran regularly, for by the One in whose hand is my soul, it slips away faster than camels escaping from their ropes."

Hadith 7: Al-Bukhari narrated from Qutaybah ibn Sa'id, from Malik ibn Anas, from Zaid ibn Aslam, from Ata ibn Yasar, from Abu Hurairah, who said: The Messenger of Allah, peace be upon him, said: "The one who recites the Quran and forgets it will meet Allah on the Day of Resurrection, and the Quran will say, 'O Lord, he recited me but forgot me.' So, strive to preserve the Quran."

Hadith 8: Al-Bukhari narrated from Muhammad ibn Sinan, from Fudayl, from Amr, from Abu Qutaybah, from Amr ibn Murrah, from Abu Burdah, from Abu Musa Al-Ash'ari, who said: The Messenger of Allah, peace be upon him, said: "Maintain the Quran, for it is more likely to escape from the hearts of men than anything else. Whoever recites it and preserves it, Allah will make it a light for him."

Commentary: These hadiths emphasize the importance of regular recitation and preservation of the Quran. The first hadith encourages reciting the Quran both openly and secretly, highlighting Allah's love for those who cherish it. The second advises against rushing through the Quran, recommending a minimum of three days for regular reciters to ensure understanding. The third distinguishes between those skilled in recitation, who are with the angels, and those who struggle, earning double rewards for their effort. The fourth and fifth hadiths stress the excellence of learning and teaching the Quran with understanding, comparing it to a garden of knowledge. The sixth, seventh, and eighth hadiths warn against forgetting the Quran, as it can slip away easily, and urge continuous practice to preserve it, as it will be a light for its reciter and a witness on the Day of Resurrection.

Etiquette of Recitation: Al-Bukhari narrated from Abu Al-Yaman, from Shu'aib, from Az-Zuhri, from Ubaydullah ibn Abdullah, from Ibn Abbas, who said: The Messenger of Allah, peace be upon him, said: "Beautify the Quran with your voices, for a beautiful voice enhances the beauty of the Quran."

Hadith 10: Al-Bukhari narrated from Abdullah ibn Yusuf, from Al-Laith, from Yazid ibn Al-Had, from Muhammad ibn Ibrahim, from Abu Salamah, from Abu Hurairah, who said: The Messenger of Allah, peace be upon him, said: "When you recite the Quran, do so with humility and reflection, and seek refuge in Allah from the accursed Satan before starting, as Allah says: 'So when you recite the Quran, seek refuge in Allah from Satan, the accursed' [An-Nahl: 98]."

Hadith 11: Al-Bukhari narrated from Qutaybah ibn Sa'id, from Malik ibn Anas, from Zaid ibn Aslam, from Ibn Umar, who said: The Messenger of Allah, peace be upon him, said: "Recite the Quran in a measured tone, and do not recite it like poetry, nor scatter it like prose, but let your hearts be moved by it."

Commentary: These hadiths outline the etiquette of Quranic recitation. The ninth encourages beautifying recitation with a pleasant voice, as it enhances the Quran's impact. The tenth emphasizes starting recitation with seeking refuge in Allah and reciting with humility and reflection. The eleventh advises a balanced, measured recitation, avoiding extremes, to ensure the heart is touched by the Quran's meanings.

The Virtue of Memorizing the Quran

Hadith 1: Al-Bukhari narrated from Muhammad ibn Al-Muthanna, from Yahya ibn Sa'id, from Shu'bah, from Qatadah, from Anas ibn Malik, who said: The Messenger of Allah, peace be upon him, said: "The one who memorizes the Quran and acts upon it will be adorned with a crown of light on the Day of

Resurrection, its light like that of the sun. His parents will be adorned with two robes better than the world and all it contains. They will say, 'Why have we been adorned like this?' It will be said, 'Because of your child's memorization of the Quran.'"

Hadith 2: Al-Bukhari narrated from Qutaybah ibn Sa'id, from Malik ibn Anas, from Zaid ibn Aslam, from Ibn Umar, who said: The Messenger of Allah, peace be upon him, said: "The one who memorizes the Quran will be told on the Day of

Resurrection: 'Recite and ascend, and recite as you used to recite in the world, for your rank will be at the last verse you recite.'"

Hadith 3: Al-Bukhari narrated from Abu Al-Yaman, from Shu'aib, from Az-Zuhri, from Salim ibn Abdullah, from Ibn Umar, who said: The Messenger of Allah, peace be upon him, said: "The Quran is a treasure, and whoever memorizes it and preserves it, Allah will raise him in rank and honor him. But whoever neglects it after memorizing it, it will be a proof against him."

Hadith 4: Al-Bukhari narrated from Abdullah ibn Yusuf, from Al-Laith, from Yazid ibn Al-Had, from Muhammad ibn Ibrahim, from Abu Salamah, from Abu Hurairah, who said: The Messenger of Allah, peace be upon him, said: "The Quran is a proof for you or against you. Whoever memorizes it and acts upon it, it will intercede for him. Whoever memorizes it and neglects it, it will testify against him on the Day of Resurrection."

Hadith 5: Al-Bukhari narrated from Muslim ibn Ibrahim, from Hisham, from Yahya ibn Abi Kathir, from Abu Salamah, from Abu Hurairah, who said: The Messenger of Allah, peace be upon him, said: "The one who memorizes the Quran will come on the Day of Resurrection, and the Quran will say, 'O Lord, intercede for him.' So, Allah will grant him intercession, and he will enter Paradise."

Hadith 6: Al-Bukhari narrated from Abu Bakr ibn Abi Shaibah, from Abu Mu'awiyah, from Al-A'mash, from Ibrahim, from Alqamah, from Abdullah ibn Mas'ud, who said:

The Messenger of Allah, peace be upon him, said: "The one who memorizes the Quran should ask Allah by it, for it is a means to draw near to Him. By the One in whose hand is my soul, the Quran is more likely to slip from the heart than a camel from its rope."

Hadith 7: Al-Bukhari narrated from Qutaybah ibn Sa'id, from Malik ibn Anas, from Zaid ibn Aslam, from Ata ibn Yasar, from Abu Hurairah, who said: The Messenger of Allah, peace be upon him, said: "Visit the Quran regularly, for it is a garden that requires tending. If you neglect it, it will fade from your heart."

Commentary: These hadiths emphasize the great virtue of memorizing the Quran and the high status of those who preserve it. The first and second hadiths highlight the rewards for memorizers, including crowns of light, elevated ranks in Paradise, and honor for their parents. The third and fourth hadiths stress that the Quran is a proof for or against its memorizer, depending on whether they act upon it. The fifth hadith shows the

Quran's intercession for its memorizer, ensuring entry to Paradise. The sixth and seventh hadiths warn against neglecting the Quran after memorization, as it can slip away easily, and urge regular review, comparing it to tending a garden or restraining a camel.

Etiquette of Memorization: Al-Bukhari narrated from Abu Al-Yaman, from Shu'aib, from Az-Zuhri, from Ubaydullah ibn Abdullah, from Ibn Abbas, who said: The Messenger of Allah, peace be upon him, said: "The one who memorizes the Quran should recite it with care and reverence, seeking Allah's pleasure, not seeking worldly gain."

Hadith 9: Al-Bukhari narrated from Abdullah ibn Yusuf, from Al-Laith, from Yazid ibn Al-Had, from Muhammad ibn Ibrahim, from Abu Salamah, from Abu Hurairah, who said: The Messenger of Allah, peace be upon him, said: "The best memorization is that which is done with sincerity for Allah, and the worst is that which is done for show or worldly reward."

Commentary: These hadiths emphasize the importance of sincerity in memorizing the Quran. Memorization should be for Allah's sake, with reverence and a desire to please Him, not for fame or material gain. This ensures the memorizer's reward and protects against hypocrisy.

On the Etiquette and Rulings Related to the Quran

Hadith 1: Al-Bukhari narrated from Qutaybah ibn Sa'id, from Malik ibn Anas, from Zaid ibn Aslam, from Ata ibn Yasar, from Abu Hurairah, who said: The Messenger of Allah, peace be upon him, said: "When you recite the Quran, seek refuge in Allah from the accursed Satan, as Allah says: 'So when you recite the

Quran, seek refuge in Allah from Satan, the accursed' [An-Nahl: 98]."

Hadith 2: Al-Bukhari narrated from Abu Al-Yaman, from Shu'aib, from Az-Zuhri, from Ubaydullah ibn Abdullah, from Ibn Abbas, who said: The Messenger of Allah, peace be upon him, said: "Beautify the Quran with your voices, for a beautiful voice enhances the beauty of the Quran. And recite it with a measured tone, for it helps in understanding its meanings."

Hadith 3: Al-Bukhari narrated from Abdullah ibn Yusuf, from Al-Laith, from Yazid ibn Al-Had, from Muhammad ibn Ibrahim, from Abu Salamah, from Abu Hurairah, who said: The Messenger of Allah, peace be upon him, said: "Do not recite the Quran loudly in a way that disturbs others, nor so quietly that you cannot hear yourself, but seek a way between them."

Hadith 4: Al-Bukhari narrated from Muhammad ibn Al-Muthanna, from Yahya ibn Sa'id, from Shu'bah, from Qatadah, from Anas ibn

Malik, who said: The Messenger of Allah, peace be upon him, said: "The best recitation is that which is done with reflection and understanding, for the Quran was revealed to be pondered over, as Allah says: 'A Book We have sent down to you, blessed, that they may reflect upon its verses' [Sad: 29]."

Hadith 5: Al-Bukhari narrated from Muslim ibn Ibrahim, from Hisham, from Yahya ibn Abi Kathir, from Abu Salamah, from Abu Hurairah, who said: The Messenger of Allah, peace be upon him, said: "When you recite the Quran, do so in a state of purity, for it is the speech of Allah, and it is not fitting to touch it except in a state of purity, as Allah says: 'None touch it except the purified' [Al-Waqi'ah: 79]."

Hadith 6: Al-Bukhari narrated from Abu Bakr ibn Abi Shaibah, from Abu Mu'awiyah, from Al-A'mash, from Ibrahim, from Alqamah, from Abdullah ibn Mas'ud, who said: The Messenger of Allah, peace be upon him, said: "Recite the Quran with humility and reverence, and let your heart be present with its meanings, for it is a cure for the hearts."

Hadith 7: Al-Bukhari narrated from Qutaybah ibn Sa'id, from Malik ibn Anas, from Zaid ibn Aslam, from Ibn Umar, who said: The Messenger of Allah, peace be upon him, said: "The Quran should be recited in a clear and distinct manner, with proper pronunciation (tajweed), for it was revealed with clarity, and its letters are counted."

Commentary: These hadiths outline the etiquette and rulings related to reciting the Quran. The first hadith emphasizes seeking refuge in Allah from Satan before recitation to ensure focus and protection. The second encourages beautifying recitation with a pleasant voice and reciting in a measured tone to aid understanding. The third advises moderation in the volume of recitation to avoid disturbing others while ensuring the reciter hears themselves. The fourth stresses the importance of reflecting on the Quran's meanings, as it was revealed for contemplation. The fifth highlights the need for ritual purity when handling or reciting the Quran, respecting its sanctity. The sixth and seventh hadiths urge reciting with humility, presence of heart, and proper pronunciation, as the Quran is a cure and must be recited clearly to preserve its integrity.

Additional Rulings: Al-Bukhari narrated from Muhammad ibn Sinan, from Fudayl, from Amr, from Abu Qutaybah, from Amr ibn Murrah, from Abu Burdah, from Abu Musa Al-Ash'ari, who said: The Messenger of Allah, peace be upon him, said: "Do not recite the Quran in the presence of those who are distracted or in a state of impurity, and do not recite it in a place where it may be disrespected."

Hadith 9: Al-Bukhari narrated from Abu Al-Yaman, from Shu'aib, from Az-Zuhri, from Salim ibn Abdullah, from Ibn Umar, who said: The Messenger of Allah, peace be upon him, said: "The Quran should not be recited in a hurried manner, like poetry, nor scattered like prose, but with care and deliberation, pausing at its wonders."

Commentary: These additional hadiths emphasize respecting the Quran's sanctity by avoiding recitation in inappropriate settings or states, such as in the presence of distraction or impurity. The ninth hadith reinforces the need for deliberate and careful recitation, pausing to reflect on the Quran's profound meanings and avoiding rushed or poetic styles that diminish its reverence.

The Virtue of Reflecting on and Acting Upon the Quran

Hadith 1: Al-Bukhari narrated from Qutaybah ibn Sa'id, from Malik ibn Anas, from Zaid ibn Aslam, from Ata ibn Yasar, from Abu Hurairah, who said: The Messenger of Allah, peace be upon him, said: "The Quran was revealed to be reflected upon, so reflect on its verses and act upon its teachings, for it is a guidance for those who believe, as Allah says: 'This is a blessed Book which We have revealed to you, that they may reflect upon its verses and that those of understanding may be reminded' [Sad: 29]."

Hadith 2: Al-Bukhari narrated from Abu Al-Yaman, from Shu'aib, from Az-Zuhri, from Ubaydullah ibn Abdullah, from Ibn Abbas, who said: The Messenger of Allah, peace be upon him, said: "The one who recites the Quran and reflects on its meanings will find light in his heart and guidance in his life. The Quran is a cure for what is in the chests."

Hadith 3: Al-Bukhari narrated from Abdullah ibn Yusuf, from Al-Laith, from Yazid ibn Al-Had, from Muhammad ibn Ibrahim, from Abu Salamah, from Abu Hurairah, who said: The Messenger of Allah, peace be upon him, said: "The best of you are those who learn the Quran, understand its meanings, and act upon it. Whoever acts upon the Quran, Allah will raise him in rank in this world and the Hereafter."

Hadith 4: Al-Bukhari narrated from Muhammad ibn Al-Muthanna, from Yahya ibn Sa'id, from Shu'bah, from Qatadah, from Anas ibn Malik, who said: The Messenger of Allah, peace be upon him, said: "The Quran is a guide and a mercy. Whoever follows its guidance will not go astray, and whoever acts upon it will be among the successful, as Allah says: 'Indeed, this Quran guides to that which is most upright' [Al-Isra: 9]."

Hadith 5: Al-Bukhari narrated from Muslim ibn Ibrahim, from Hisham, from Yahya ibn Abi Kathir, from Abu Salamah, from Abu Hurairah, who said: The Messenger of Allah, peace be upon him, said: "The one who recites the Quran but does not act upon it is like a blind man who carries a lamp—it benefits others but not himself."

Hadith 6: Al-Bukhari narrated from Abu Bakr ibn Abi Shaibah, from Abu Mu'awiyah, from Al-A'mash, from Ibrahim, from Alqamah, from Abdullah ibn Mas'ud, who said: The Messenger of Allah, peace be upon him, said: "Do not be among those who recite the Quran but neglect its commands. The Quran will testify against those who recite it without acting upon it on the Day of Resurrection."

Hadith 7: Al-Bukhari narrated from Qutaybah ibn Sa'id, from Malik ibn Anas, from Zaid ibn Aslam, from Ibn Umar, who said: The Messenger of Allah, peace be upon him, said: "The Quran is a responsibility. Whoever takes it upon himself to understand and act upon it, Allah will make it a means of honor for him. Whoever turns away from it, it will be a burden against him."

Commentary: These hadiths emphasize the importance of reflecting on the Quran's meanings and applying its teachings in daily life. The first and second hadiths highlight that the Quran was revealed for reflection, serving as a source of light, guidance, and healing for the heart. The third and fourth hadiths stress that true excellence lies in learning, understanding, and acting upon the Quran, which leads to success and elevated ranks. The fifth and sixth hadiths warn against reciting the Quran without acting on it, comparing such a person to a blind man carrying a lamp, and note that the Quran will testify against those who neglect its commands. The seventh hadith underscores the Quran as a responsibility, bringing honor to those who uphold it and a burden to those who ignore it.

Additional Guidance on Reflection: Al-Bukhari narrated from Muhammad ibn Sinan, from Fudayl, from Amr, from Abu

Qutaybah, from Amr ibn Murrah, from Abu Burdah, from Abu Musa Al-Ash'ari, who said: The Messenger of Allah, peace be upon him, said: "Reflect on the Quran with your hearts, for it is a reminder for those who reflect, and act upon it, for it is a guide for those who follow."

Hadith 9: Al-Bukhari narrated from Abu Al-Yaman, from Shu'aib, from Az-Zuhri, from Salim ibn Abdullah, from Ibn Umar, who said: The Messenger of Allah, peace be upon him, said: "The one who recites the

Quran and ponders its meanings will find his heart softened and his deeds purified, for the Quran is a purifier for those who reflect."

Commentary: These additional hadiths reinforce the need for heartfelt reflection on the Quran, which softens the heart, purifies deeds, and serves as a reminder and guide for those who ponder its verses. Acting upon the Quran is essential to fully benefit from its guidance and blessings.

Various Other Hadiths

Hadith 1: Al-Bukhari narrated from Qutaybah ibn Sa'id, from Malik ibn Anas, from Zaid ibn Aslam, from Ata ibn Yasar, from Abu Hurairah, who said: The Messenger of Allah, peace be upon him, said: "The Quran is a proof for you or against you. Whoever recites it, understands it, and acts upon it will find it as an intercessor on the Day of Resurrection. Whoever neglects it after knowing it will find it as a witness against him."

Hadith 2: Al-Bukhari narrated from Abu Al-Yaman, from Shu'aib, from Az-Zuhri, from Ubaydullah ibn Abdullah, from Ibn Abbas, who said: The Messenger of Allah, peace be upon him, said: "The one who recites the Quran and excels in its recitation will be with the noble angels. The one who recites it with difficulty, striving to improve, will have two rewards."

Hadith 3: Al-Bukhari narrated from Abdullah ibn Yusuf, from Al-Laith, from Yazid ibn Al-Had, from Muhammad ibn Ibrahim, from Abu Salamah, from Abu Hurairah, who said: The Messenger of Allah, peace be upon him, said: "The Quran is a garden of knowledge and a river of wisdom. Whoever drinks from it will be purified, and whoever turns away from it will be wretched."

Hadith 4: Al-Bukhari narrated from Muhammad ibn Al-Muthanna, from Yahya ibn Sa'id, from Shu'bah, from Qatadah, from Anas ibn Malik, who said: The Messenger of Allah, peace be upon him, said:

"The Quran is a light in the heart and a guide on the path. Whoever holds fast to it will not be misguided, as Allah says: 'Indeed, this Quran guides to that which is most upright' [Al-Isra: 9]."

Hadith 5: Al-Bukhari narrated from Muslim ibn Ibrahim, from Hisham, from Yahya ibn Abi Kathir, from Abu Salamah, from Abu Hurairah, who said: The Messenger of Allah, peace be upon him, said: "The Quran will come to its companion on the Day of Resurrection like a friend, saying, 'O Lord, I was recited by this person, so grant him honor.' And Allah will honor him."

Hadith 6: Al-Bukhari narrated from Abu Bakr ibn Abi Shaibah, from Abu Mu'awiyah, from Al-A'mash, from Ibrahim, from Alqamah, from Abdullah ibn Mas'ud, who said: The Messenger of Allah, peace be upon him, said: "The Quran is a trust from Allah. Whoever takes it upon himself to recite it and follow it, Allah will make it a means of salvation for him. Whoever abandons it, it will be a regret for him."

Commentary: These hadiths summarize the overarching virtues of the Quran. The first and second hadiths reiterate the Quran's role as a proof or intercessor, rewarding those who recite it proficiently or with effort. The third and fourth hadiths describe the Quran as a source of knowledge, wisdom, and guidance, purifying those who engage with it and warning against neglecting it. The fifth hadith emphasizes the Quran's companionship on the Day of Resurrection, advocating for its reciter. The sixth hadith presents the Quran as a divine trust, bringing salvation to those who uphold it and regret to those who abandon it.

Conclusion: Al-Bukhari narrated from Qutaybah ibn Sa'id, from Malik ibn Anas, from Zaid ibn Aslam, from Ibn Umar, who said: The Messenger of Allah, peace be upon him, said: "The Quran is the speech of Allah, revealed to His Prophet, peace be upon him, as a guidance for mankind. Whoever recites it, reflects on it, and acts upon it will find it as a light in this world and a companion in the Hereafter. Whoever turns away from it will find darkness in his heart and loss in the Hereafter."

Final Remarks by Ibn Kathir: The virtues of the Quran are numerous, as it is the eternal miracle of the Prophet, peace be upon him, and the foundation of guidance for the Muslim community. Its recitation brings reward, its memorization elevates ranks, its reflection purifies hearts, and its application leads to success in both worlds. The Quran is a trust and a responsibility, and those who uphold it are honored by Allah. May Allah make us among those who recite, memorize, understand, and act upon His Book, and may He protect us from neglecting it. And all praise is due to Allah, Lord of the worlds.

www.ingramcontent.com/pod-product-compliance
Lightning Source LLC
Chambersburg PA
CBHW050113170426
43198CB00014B/2562